Flow Series **BOOK 1**

FIND YOUR flow

THRIVE UNDER PRESSURE

LEON BAX Ph.D.

2MYNDS BOOKS
Unleash Your Mind
Visit us at www.2mynds.com/books/

FIND YOUR FLOW

Printed in the United States of America
Published by 2Mynds, Inc.
ISBN: 979-8-9888996-1-7 (Paperback)
Illustrations by Fernanda da Costa and Leon Bax
Psychology, fitness, mental health, meditation

"To the mind that is still, the whole universe surrenders."

Lao Tzu

TABLE OF CONTENTS

ACKNOWLEDGMENTS

I have so many vivid memories of exceptional encounters that I would have to write a book in and of itself to do them justice. Maybe, someday, that will happen. For now, I would like to acknowledge everyone who has inspired me on my journey. Whether you fired me up or tried to slam the brakes, you helped me choose my path, and you are still reflecting on it. Please keep it coming!

PREFACE

When I was born, I looked so small and fragile that the doctors put me in an incubator for a day. I remained small for my age, and my father began taking me to Judo lessons when I was four. I am sure he thought it would come in handy in the schoolyards. I do not remember being bullied, but I learned how to turn being small into an advantage at an early age.

When I was 10, my father took me to a Judo tournament that, at the time, seemed like any other tournament. I remember the boy I fought in the finals - the same boy who had beaten me a few weeks before – and I remember the throw that won me the fight. I even remember the smell of the mat and the gymnasium. At some point during the car ride home, I checked out my trophy, upon which my father asked: "What does it say?" I read it out loud: "First place, National Championships Boys 25kg". As I said it, I still didn't realize what I had won. I was admiring the trophy. My dad smiled, and later, my mom spelled it out for me.

The memory of my father on that day has always stuck in my mind. Even though it was a national tournament, he created an atmosphere where I could be present and absorb everything around me. He made me feel free to do what I had trained to do instead of making me concerned with winning or losing. I believe his unusual approach fostered my ability to focus intensely on actions themselves rather than on their consequences.

I have been extremely fortunate to have had these experiences early in life. They taught me that the big deal with competing wasn't in the result but in the depth of the experience. While I had my share of doubts and struggles, profound experiences continued, and they proved a critical point: obstacles are the facilitators of profound experiences. If you want your learnings to stick, obstacles are your ally.

I have led a life in which I sought out my obstacles, and sometimes they sought me out. This is true for my personal life, academic career, business ventures, sports, and even health. A notable event, one that put me on the road towards building a mental fitness startup and writing this book, happened on a seemingly unfortunate day in early 2017. After an infection that I had developed on a trip abroad, my immune system had gone haywire, and my kidneys and liver had started to shut down. Doctors told me I needed surgery on my arms if I didn't want to lose them entirely. There was no general treatment for the condition except intravenous fluids and time. Around midnight that day, I remember telling the orthopedic surgeon not to operate until the next morning to see if I would be doing better. He wasn't happy and asked me if I had a will. Somehow, I felt strangely calm and resolved and focused on one thing and nothing else: giving my body the best chance to heal. When I asked the nurse if there was a quiet yoga or meditation room, I remember her saying jokingly: "You are not going to do any exercise, young man – it is bad for your health!"

For the next few hours, I alternated relaxation techniques with emotional projections of being blissed out. When they took my blood at 5:00 in the morning, there were minor signs of improvement. The surgeon agreed to postpone surgery and see if the test results would continue to get better. This pattern repeated for a few days until my head was clear and my body felt normal. When I left the hospital, while weak physically, I felt invigorated and determined.

During my recovery, I re-evaluated my priorities in life and realized that I had wandered away from a path I had been on when I was younger. I had strayed because it was more convenient and socially acceptable. In the process, I had foregone the opportunity, and perhaps the obligation, to integrate many unique teachings I had received into my own life and the lives of others. As I was discharged from the hospital and recovered further at home, I negotiated a reduction of my hours at my regular job and decided to turn the lights in my brain back on (or rather, open the curtains). This book is the inevitable result of that process.

As books go, it is full of words, unsurprisingly. Some words may resonate with you, and some others may not. Therefore, and this may sound like a contradiction, the eventual goal of this book is to lead you away from the words to the intent and emotion behind them. Then, ultimately, I hope to guide you toward a practice.

Even though mental training has become a buzzword, especially in sports, not many people realize the misnomer. Counseling sessions in the comfort of an office are, by definition, not training. Unfortunately, functional workouts that are periodized and progressive are rare in clinical or sports settings. Even most professional athletes still don't work their minds with multi-week training programs similar to programs they use for physical fitness. These are the same athletes who push themselves endlessly in the gym, knowing that the discomfort is essential for progress.

We need a paradigm shift in mental health, and the Flow Series aims to inspire you to be part of that. For everything the books cannot cover, particularly getting your reps in, the Flow 255® online platform [1] is there for you. Think of the book as the 30,000-foot view from the sky and the platform as your GPS on the ground. You can work with either or both of them. Welcome to the journey!

Leon Bax, November 2023

Chapter 1

A ROAD BEYOND KNOWLEDGE

"It is not what you know that makes a difference. It is what you do with your knowledge."

Understanding Is Not Enough

Knowledge is power. This simple adage has become accepted wisdom everywhere, from the boardroom to the work floor, as well as in schools, sports clubs, and music halls. And it is true, as far as it goes. Competitive athletes, coaches, and trainers appreciate that comprehensive knowledge of challenges and solutions can be a foundation for peak performance. But they have also witnessed hundreds if not thousands of examples where someone knew exactly what to do yet didn't execute accordingly. In other words, knowing what to do and actually doing it are two different things. Even knowledge by itself has its limitations. No less of a wise man than Socrates once told another man in ancient Greece:

> *"Although I do not suppose that either*
> *of us knows anything, I am better off than*
> *he is, for he knows nothing and thinks*
> *that he knows – I neither know nor think*
> *that I know."* [2]

Socrates was right. Knowledge, whether in life, work, school, or sports, is limited by the framework it was conceived in, so it is better to assume you don't know anything for sure. Knowledge, as it lives in our brain, is based on neural activity patterns that represent memories and anticipations that flow from them based on rudimentary logic. As such, it is, by definition, colored by our experience and mental faculties. Although understanding our limitations is the starting point for finding wisdom, our logic and analytics can severely interfere with peak presence and performance.

Being analytical means being divisive (the original meaning of the word analysis is "to take apart"). For this reason, being analytical is never a wholesome experience. It breaks up connections and detaches from reality, which is helpful at times, but when decisive action is required, it can freeze you up: paralysis by analysis. [3] On the other hand, being observant means you are inclusive – your mind is open. Not surprisingly, observing deeply is associated with a vastly different brain state than thinking deeply, with similarly disparate effects on our physiology. [4] This has important implications for mental exercises; we will return to this later.

Many athletes and coaches instinctively understand that knowledge and skills play different roles in physical training. For example, everyone agrees that knowing how to perform a deadlift does not mean you can actually do it. Thus, personal trainers optimize physical fitness via exercises, training plans, and explicitly planned periodic progressions (periodizations). [5] However, in mental health, the fitness aspect tends to get ignored, and the idea of periodization of mental workouts, or even the concept of mental workouts themselves, is still foreign to many mental health professionals and their clients.

Mental Fitness and Mental Health

Mental fitness is a broad concept central to this book, so let's define what it is and isn't. Mental or physical fitness refers to the ability to perform tasks related to day-to-day activities. [6] As an ability, fitness is not an activity. You *are* a level of fit; you don't *do* a level of fit. The doing part of fitness is what we call training.

As a capacity to execute tasks, fitness contributes to health but does not exclusively determine it. Health is a more expansive concept than fitness. For example, you can be physically fit, with tremendous physical skills on a tennis court, ski slope, or surfboard (based on attributes such as endurance, strength, and agility), but you can still catch a cold and develop pneumonia. Similarly, you can have excellent mental skills, such as remaining calm and relaxed under pressure when giving a speech, stepping up to bat in baseball, or free climbing a wall (with attributes such as determination, motivation, and confidence). However, you can still have post-traumatic stress disorder.

Figure 1. Mental health and mental fitness

Recognizing the Challenges

Although mental fitness logically deserves the same attention as physical fitness, several factors have prevented organized training for mental fitness from taking off:

1. Getting help from psychologists or mental coaches often carries a social stigma, especially for children and young adults, and is still seen as a sign of weakness.
2. Psychologists are seen as professionals who treat problems. Very few people go to psychologists to prevent problems.

3. Mental support interventions are often wrongfully perceived as mental training. Support is something you receive in comfort; training is something you do in discomfort.
4. Psychologists tend to work in offices and clinics. This means that the conditions under which the interventions take place are not representative of the conditions of the applications.
5. The confrontational nature of self-reflection and meditative training often invokes a tendency to avoid such practices.
6. Human beings tend to follow the path of least resistance. Becoming mentally fit requires effort, and compliance with a mental exercise regimen that pushes boundaries is low without proper guidance.
7. For mental workouts to be effective, they must follow common training principles from exercise science. Until now, thorough methodology and user-friendly technology that integrate exercise physiology into behavioral psychology have been missing.
8. Due to the lack of explicit training methodologies, most psychology curriculums do not teach mental workout design and periodization.

These challenges are the root of the motivation to write this book series. Each issue will be addressed along the way.

Chapter summary. Knowing what to do is only a small part of fulfilling your life. It's what you do that makes a difference. Mental health is one of the critical determinants of what you can and cannot do in your life. Mental fitness is an under-addressed component of mental health, and this book introduces a practical approach to developing and maintaining mental fitness.

Lost in translation. Knowledge is not stored in our brain as individual words or thoughts. Instead, our brain works in patterns that represent concepts. This is for reasons of efficiency as well as generalizability. It is much like explaining a landscape to someone with words – it could take all day. Instead, you could just show a picture and be done in a second.

Although our brain works in patterns, when we communicate with others, we tend to do so verbally. Consequently, every pattern or concept in our brain must be translated into words. We do this predominantly with our brain's left hemisphere.[7] Next, whoever listens to our words must translate them back into patterns. As you can imagine, things get lost and misunderstood in this process: the sender may not have chosen the right words, and the receiver may misinterpret some of them.

There are two important takeaways. First, in any communication that matters to you, don't get hung up on words. Find the intent and meaning that created them and respond to that, verbally or non-verbally. Second, if you want to make changes to your life, you have to walk your talk. So it's not about what you understand. It's what you do with that understanding.

Chapter 2

PROGRESS TO STRESS

"Stressors are external,
but stress is internal and
of your own making."

The Mental Fallacy

Everything that affects your physiology, particularly your blood chemistry, will affect your brain. Your brain is a physical organ, just like your heart, liver, and muscles. Not only that, but your brain is also a primary regulator of the physiology that it is affected by. In other words, your brain regulates not only your body but also itself.

Let's have a look at an example. When you engage in physical activity, your brain and nervous system increase your heart rate and blood pressure. Your nervous system will also initiate a cascade of actions that changes your hormonal balance and your blood's biochemical profile. But here is the kicker: the adjusted availability of neurotransmitters that is orchestrated by your brain optimizes its own alertness. In fact, almost every action your brain undertakes will affect itself. As organisms, we function and survive by the grace of these feedback loops that do not discriminate between mind and body. The moral of the story? It is ignorant to separate mind and body when optimizing presence and performance in life.

The Nervous System in Action

Most of us would agree that our body is the most remarkable biochemical factory on the planet. However, this factory needs good leadership, and that is where our nervous system comes in, with our brain as its command center. The secret to our nervous system's power lies in its building blocks: nerve cells, which are flexible and adaptive, meaning they'll adjust to challenges (neuroplasticity).

The highest density of nerve cells is found in the brain. While our spinal cord contains nerve cell bodies as well, it is also the home of many strains of nerve cell extensions. It is via these extensions that nerve cells send and receive information. The brain and the spinal cord comprise the central nervous system or CNS - your command center. Your brain is its headquarters, and the extensions that reach out into the periphery of your body are like a network of high-speed cables that carry all the information to and from the headquarters. This external network is also known as your peripheral nervous system or PNS.

CENTRAL NERVOUS SYSTEM	PERIPHERAL NERVOUS SYSTEM
Brain & Spinal Cord	Nerves & Nerve Endings
The command center	The messengers

Figure 2. The roles of the central and peripheral nervous system

The level of awareness is a critical piece of how these nervous systems work. Besides the common distinction of aware or unaware, it is helpful to consider some processes sub-aware: you may typically be unaware, but they can be brought to awareness. Let's take, for example, an autonomous (automatic) process like keeping a postural balance. Typically, you are unaware of everything that goes into your balance - you simply stay upright - but because it is a subaware process, you can bring much of it to your awareness with the proper attention. Some autonomous processes are easier to bring to awareness than others. For example, bringing your breathing motion to your awareness is more straightforward than doing that for your heart rate. A step up from there is blood flow and blood pressure.

One of the premises of this book series is that a significant issue preventing us from tapping into the deeper powers of our mind is that we tend to work only with things in our awareness. You will see that processes of which we are unaware can be brought to our awareness for a specific period so that we can explore them, work with them, and even direct them. After that, we can let them fall back into our subawareness, now enriched by our training. Many of the techniques covered later will use this concept.

Muscle Tone

Human beings consist mainly (60 percent) of water. In fact, our brain, heart, and lungs are closer to 80 percent. [8] Water has no shape, so we need something to give all that water form: bones. Our bones are our most rudimentary source of structure. However, they are stiff and static. Luckily, by design or by glorious accident, we have multiple bones kept together by joints. To further our luck, the joints have contractive tissue around them, putting us in a whole new ball game of functionality: locomotion!

The contractive tissue mentioned above is, of course, our muscles. Muscles are incredibly complex organs that take care of movement and work constantly to regulate our posture and reactivity. To fulfill these primary functions, our muscles need tension – not too much, not too little and this is often referred to as muscle tone. Muscle tone is a function of many factors, for example, your general health, the circadian rhythm (i.e., time of day), fatigue, and the state of excitement of your central nervous system. Although muscle tone is crucial for peak performance in sports, there is a mental equivalent that plays an equally critical role: alertness.

Muscle tone and alertness create what we will refer to as base tension: the physical and mental components of our reactiveness. Base tension regulates reflexes, posture, balance, and accuracy of movements. Too little or too much base tension will adversely affect your performance as an athlete: too little can slow reactions, and too much can impair the efficiency and effectiveness of movements. The primary regulator of base tension is our central nervous system. Based on signals from the environment, the brain decides on optimal alertness and muscle tension. When base tension increases in intensity and becomes uncomfortable, we give it a different name: stress.

The Nature of Stress

When your central nervous system decides your base tension is insufficient to deal with a challenge, a so-called acute stress response is set in motion. [9] This initial reaction is coordinated by the sympathetic adreno-medullar (SAM) axis, i.e., your amygdala and adrenal glands. This involves a rush of epinephrine (adrenaline), and the resulting reaction can be so fast that the body may react before you have cognitively understood its cause. [10] This initial stress response should be cherished because, without it, you would not be capable of surviving sudden challenges to your well-being. Immediately after this initial reaction, your hypothalamus (your hormonal command center) and your pituitary and adrenal glands, the hypothalamus-pituitary-adrenal (HPA) axis, can sustain stress via stress hormones such as cortisol. This ensures you stay alert long enough to fight, retreat, and find a place to recover.

Typically, after dealing with a stressor, the stress hormone levels normalize, and with it, our base tension. However, in our modern world, an abundance of stimuli get added to our already full plate of challenges, and before we know it, our mind and body remain on high alert. The high levels of stress hormones not only cause a plethora of medical issues but also result in a higher base tension. With that higher base tension, the threshold for minor stimuli to set off an acute stress reaction is much lower, creating the false impression that our acute stress response is no longer our friend. However, it is not our acute stress response that is the culprit, but rather our inability to modulate our base tension, resulting in sustained stress hormones.

For example, assume you are studying for an exam, caught a cold, and haven't slept well. When your sister asks if you can walk the dog, you snap at her and tell her she's always trying to get you to do stuff for her. Under normal circumstances, you might have seen walking the dog as something fun, but because your base tension is high, you may react emotionally to something that would otherwise not cause a stress reaction. As a consequence, your stress reaction is prolonged and can get into a vicious cycle. However, with the proper training, you learn to adjust your base tension or break vicious cycles due to increased adrenaline resistance.

The Physiology of Excitement

Although stress tends to have a bad rep, the reaction in and of itself is neither positive nor negative. Interestingly, the physiology of stress and excitement are very similar.

Let's say you are in a restaurant, and a famous actress walks in. She sits at a table beside you and starts a fun conversation with you. That might excite you and make you feel cheerful and thrilled. Alternatively, she might start an argument with the person she is dining with and get aggressive when you glance at her. In both cases, you might knock over your glass of wine for the same reason: your body is tense, your movements are clumsy, your hands are sweating, you have tunnel vision, and you aren't thinking straight. Your heart rate, blood pressure, and breathing patterns are also similar. Even your blood chemistry, including stress hormones and other mediators of alertness, are virtually identical in stress and excitement.

The similarity of our physiology under stress and in excitement has been studied extensively. It turns out that much of our experience depends on how our brain interprets the stimuli. The same stimulus can make us feel scared or excited, depending on how we look at it. This forms the basis of a treatment called anxiety reappraisal therapy.[11] The takeaway is that our perspectives allow us to transform a seemingly harmful event into an exciting one.

Triggers

When it comes to triggers for excitement or stress, the spectrum includes situational, mental, and physical triggers. Situational triggers are external circumstances. They are perceived, aware or unaware, and classified as challenges to your status quo. For example, a potential threat to your well-being will put your mind and body at heightened alertness so you can cope better. Common situational triggers of stress reactions are environmental changes that cause sensations of extreme pressure, temperature, tastes, and smells.

While some situational triggers will cause an immediate stress response that could almost be considered a reflex, other triggers are slower and more mediated by experience and expectations. It is essential to recognize that for all situational triggers, the ultimate cause of stress is not the situation but the interpretation of it - the thoughts and emotions your brain engages in. This means that whether situational changes become a trigger for a stress response depends on our cognitive engagement. Most people rarely train this capacity of their brain and subsequently feel they can't help but get stressed by what is happening around them.

Mental triggers can also occur by themselves and are commonly thoughts and emotions. Our brain is always looking for ways to simplify its activity and store patterns instead of individual pieces of information. If negative thoughts or emotions are repeated often, they can become patterns and mental triggers of a stress response. On the other hand, our brain constantly replaces patterns as it is learning, and it can do the same for mental patterns that trigger a stress response.

While mental triggers of stress tend to receive less attention than situational triggers, physical or movement triggers tend to get overlooked. Physical activity, by very definition, changes the physiological status quo of a human body. Suppose the physical activity is strenuous and challenging. Our heart rate, blood pressure, and base tension go up, and our physical and emotional reactiveness are prioritized over cognitive reactiveness. Interestingly, when the activity is planned and voluntary, acute stress tends to be interpreted as exciting, and people do not feel stressed, even though physiologically, the biochemistry is the same.

Finally, perhaps the most intriguing aspect of triggers is not their variety but rather the consistency of the reaction to them. It turns out that it doesn't matter if a trigger was situational, mental, or physical - the physiology of the acute stress reaction is nearly identical. This opens the possibility of deliberately using triggers to progress stress levels in mental workouts. We will cover this in detail later. For now, it's sufficient to understand that acute stress reactions are not just necessary; depending on the interpretation, they can even feel good!

When Tense Makes Sense

Now that we know that something that makes you feel tight under one circumstance can make you feel excited under another, it's time to see when feeling tense makes sense. This depends on many factors, and the optimal tension for one task may be too much for another. To optimize our base tension as well as our stress reaction, several tension-related skills are important:

1. Gauging rising tension levels early. For example, some people may only start noticing excess tension after it builds up to the point of no return (with stress levels so high they are harder to reduce).
2. Learning which tension levels match which performance requirements. For example, a rising

tension level may be labeled as negative because of some discomfort, but it may be optimal and necessary for the task that is about to be performed.

3. Regulating tension levels. For example, when tension is above or below what is optimal, techniques to bring the tension down are not sufficiently trained to work under stress.

So, as we get to training our mental skills, studying tension rather than running away from it is a crucial first step towards learning to recognize which levels of stress are functional or dysfunctional. The only way to do this safely and playfully is to purposefully expose ourselves to gradually increasing levels of stress. Adventure sports and martial arts are activities where this occurs naturally, but typically not to cultivate mental skills, and they also lack the methodology for purposefully moderating and progressing the stress levels.

Quick summary. From the vantage point of human physiology, your mind and body cannot be separated. The acute stress response is nearly identical under various triggers and the difference between feeling stressed or excited can depend on your state of mind and interpretation of the situation at hand. To perform under pressure, you must train under pressure, and physical exercise can be used to emulate and regulate a controlled acute stress response for training purposes.

The players in your brain. The human brain has many parts that play a role in athletes' peak performance. Without being exhaustive, the five main players are your brain stem (for homeostasis), your cerebellum (for movement foundations), your hypothalamus (for initiation), your amygdala (for emotions), and your prefrontal cortex (for cognitive processes). These parts have strong connections and can either inhibit or increase the activity of the other parts and of themselves.

An example of inhibitive impact is the amygdala reducing prefrontal cortex and cerebellum activity. For example, when you are angry, you tend to think less clearly, and your fine motor skills suffer. Conversely, cerebral activity during extensive thinking interferes with coordinated muscle activations: try to solve a complex math problem while you balance a stick on your finger.

The communication between the various parts of your brain takes place at an autonomous level—meaning you are unaware of it, and there are limitations to your influence. This is common for almost all life-sustaining activities that your brain coordinates. These activities can be classified as activating or deactivating. Although much of it is beyond your voluntary control, you can influence some of this autonomic activity by using your body. For example, although it may be hard to bring our heart rate down by sheer willpower, you can use breathing techniques to affect your heart via a body-to-body loop.

Chapter 3

A FIRST FLOW

"Flow is not something that is on or off. It has levels, and you regulate it with a dial, not a switch."

Flow

The term flow, as it relates to performance and enjoyment, was brought to the mainstream by Hungarian-American psychologist Mihaly Csikszentmihalyi. As a young child, towards the end of World War II, Csikszentmihalyi was intrigued by people capable of achieving happiness and creativity under dire circumstances. He moved to the US to study psychology and eventually became a renowned researcher and thought leader on positive psychology.[12]

Csikszentmihalyi considered flow "a transient mental state in which a person is highly focused and fully engaged in the situation or activity at hand." Based on thousands of interviews with successful athletes, scientists, artists, and other individuals who excelled at their craft, he identified nine conditions of flow, with the first three being so-called antecedents and the last six being characteristics:

Antecedents
1. Clear goals
2. Balance between skills and challenges
3. Unambiguous feedback

Characteristics
1. Focused attention
2. Merging of action and awareness
3. Sense of control
4. Lack of self-consciousness
5. Distortion of time
6. Internal commitment

Csikszentmihalyi's conditions indicate that people who set clear goals more easily achieve fulfillment in their lives and find flow in their performance. However, unlike how most people use goals, people who tend to flow easily have a level of detachment from those goals. It is as if they use them as a directive while getting the actual fulfillment from the act of going after the goals. Csikszentmihalyi called this an autotelic experience - deriving purpose (telos) from itself (autos). Some psychologists believe this tendency is associated with personality types. More about this later.

A Critical Look at Flow

All three antecedents point to flow being associated with (the challenge of) tasks. Csikszentmihalyi operationalized this with a flow quadrant:

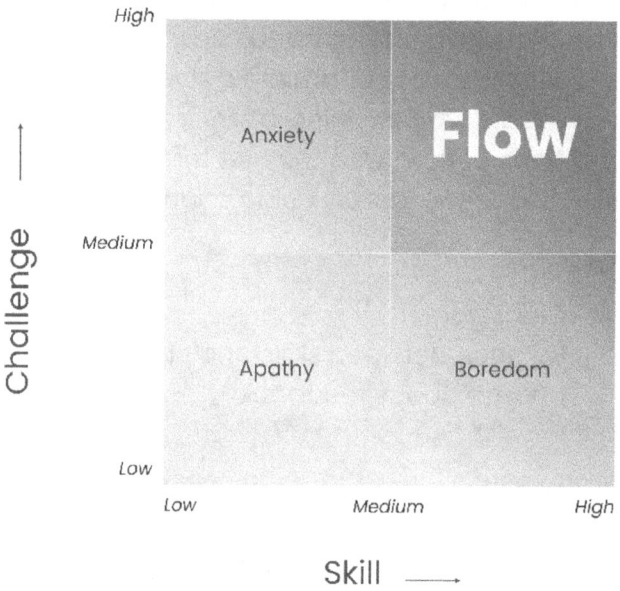

Figure 3. The flow quadrant

The quadrant indicates that in situations where a task poses no challenge and someone has a low skill level for that particular task (lower left), the resulting state of mind trends toward apathy. When the challenge is minimal, but someone's skill level is high (lower right), they tend to be bored. When challenges far exceed someone's skills (upper left), the situation results in fear and anxiety. Finally, flow occurs most easily when challenges are high, but the skills to cope with them are also extensive (upper right). Interestingly, this idea of conditions for flow and the skill-challenge balance shown in the flow quadrant goes against the notion of autotelic experiences.

In an autotelic experience, as Csikszentmihalyi himself describes it, the activity itself provides everything that is needed to motivate the engagement in it. If that is true, an autotelic experience or personality requires no antecedents to flow (because the action itself suffices as motivation to engage fully). This actually makes sense from a meditative perspective.

Flow experiences tend to be very common in meditative practices, particularly those that focus on sensory impressions (more on that in the next chapter). Most meditative practices have an autotelic tendency in that nothing is forced or pursued. It's easy to see that this contrasts with Csikszentmihalyi's antecedents:

1. No clear goals are required.
2. It does not have to be challenging.
3. Ambiguity stimulates exploration.

Another issue with the common interpretation of Csikszentmihalyi's definition of flow is the notion that in flow, "everything goes your way effortlessly." This is a commercialized interpretation that misses the mark. While the "effortless achievement" sells, no achievement comes without effort. You can experience an incredible feeling of flow and unity when you sit along the ocean shore or walk in a forest. In these situations, flow is not there because all the antecedents are there but because there is a certain level of unattached awareness. Because most people experience flow by accident, not by design, very few realize its nuances and idiosyncrasies. Hence, the idea that you are either "in it or not" is widely accepted. Unfortunately, nothing could be further from the truth.

An Alternative Definition

Let's take a closer look at the unattached awareness in many meditative practices, particularly mindful meditation: aware but unattached means you are observing but not lingering on what you observe. In other words, you are in each moment without your awareness going to past moments or future moments – without lingering in time. This detaching or delingering can only happen when your sensory perception is managed appropriately by your attention in time and space. The above two sentences carry a profound meaning. In a way, you could say that this entire book serves to clarify these statements and make them practical and impactful. Let's start by redefining flow:

> *"Flow is a multi-level experience of the present in which a person is connected but unattached to sentient focus."*

This definition indicates that flow has levels (multi-level) and is based on a profound sensory experience (connected, sentient) of continuously refreshing time and space (unattached presence). It is not a singular state that you are in or not but rather a continuity of states through which you can progress. In other words, flow has no switch – it has a dial. The key to flow is connecting but not attaching to an object of attentive focus. That requires the ability to control attention at an advanced level: to not only focus it on the present but also divide it and be both observer and observed. Defining flow in a way that relates it to abilities brings it to the realm of training (away from antecedents and hoping for the best). This idea of training brings us to attributes and skills.

Mental Attributes

Mental attributes are psychological qualities. They are things you have, not things you do. Mental attributes can have cognitive variations, such as perspectives, convictions, or beliefs, and emotional variations, such as positive and negative emotions. For example, someone might have a profoundly positive outlook on competing and battling with an adversary. This is cognitive and rational, but it also has an emotional component: feelings of gratitude and anticipatory excitement to compete.

Attributes can be self-supportive, like confidence, gratitude, and courage, but they can also be self-limiting, like stubbornness, anxiousness, fearfulness, and pride. They can even be dormant, waiting to be triggered. Manifestations of mental attributes can change from one moment to the other, and their stability depends on how well they have been cultivated under pressure. You may be grateful when things go your way, but for most of us, it is much harder to see the gift of an experience when that experience is challenging.

How does this relate to flow? It's pretty simple: if you cultivate the right perspectives and you can control your positive emotions, you have the right mental conditions to go deeper into the moment (into flow). We have identified five attributes that are of crucial importance for mental fitness, and we'll address each in detail later on.

Mental Skills

While having the right attributes is helpful for your mental fitness, it is not enough to make you mentally fit. To translate attributes to function, you need skills. Mental skills are very different from mental attributes: they are abilities that change with training and input, not qualities that are present or triggered. Let's take attributes such as emotional states or beliefs. You can go from grateful to annoyed from one moment to the other. Or from confident to full of doubt. But you can't trigger a skill: you don't become good or bad at relaxing in an instant. You have to train your ability to relax, and if you fail to get your reps in, your relaxation skills will fail to serve you when it matters.

While attributes require cultivation through exposure, skills need training. Skills also imply activity towards a function, an "-ing" rather than a state. This may seem obvious, but much of what is referred to as mental training in the psychology and sports psychology literature is mislabeled and would not be considered training from the perspective of exercise science. Watching a video or reading a book (including this one) isn't training. Getting counseling isn't training. Keeping a journal isn't training, except perhaps for your writing skills and analytical abilities. And even doing a meditation in the morning isn't necessarily training. That doesn't mean these activities are not helpful or do not develop essential insights. They lack, however, the requisite steps that generate a physiological adaptation response that will generate functional changes in mental skills. We will cover this later on in detail. First, we take a look at what can be learned from meditative practices in terms of cultivating attributes and training skills.

> **Quick summary.** Flow is a multi-level state. It is dialed up and down, not switched on or off. Replicating it requires mental mental fitness and is not simply a matter of setting the right conditions. Mental fitness depends on mental attributes and skills that in turn require functional training.

Words of flow. Flow is only one of many words that can be used to describe the state or feeling that is commonly associated with it. The concept has many nuances, depending on the context, but it is interesting to see that there are commonalities across psychology, sports, music, business, and even governance.

Peak Experience is an expression that Abraham Maslow used to describe "transient moments of self-actualization." [13] Maslow studied human motivation and placed self-actualization at its epicenter, typically after more fundamental needs were addressed. He considered peak experiences attainable for everyone, but not everyone would have them with equal frequency, awareness, or appreciation.

In the Zone appears to have its origins in sports. Tennis player Arthur Ashe used the expression in a 1974 audio diary entry describing the way Bjorn Borg played in their match in London. [14] "Borg beat me 6-4, 7-6 tonight, and he is in what we call the zone." He used it as a reference to The Twilight Zone series and explained it meant "Playing as if from another world."

The Ideal Performance State (IPS) was originally defined by psychologist James Loehr, [15] and he described it as a psychological state in which high energy and positive feelings intersect. It is based on physical, emotional, mental, and spiritual capacities that must work in unison to produce a state in which performance is optimized.

Wu Wei (無為) is an ancient Chinese expression that means inaction or (perhaps more accurately) unforced action. [16] It refers to a personal level of free-flowing harmony with inner and outer nature. It has its origins in Confucianism and became a pillar of Taoist thought. The ideas were applied to life, government, and leadership.

Chapter 4

MEDITATION

"A life of meditation is meaningless if you can't be meditative in life."

What Is Meditation?

The word meditation has its roots in Latin: the verb *meditare* means to ponder or reflect, and this is a good start for a general definition: "to reflect on yourself." In fact, the Roman emperor Marcus Aurelius wrote a book titled" Meditations,"[17] which is literally a composition of reflections on life, society, and being an emperor.

Reflection implies observing from a distance, usually the past or future. To reflect on yourself, you must be both the observer and the observed. The practical implication of this can be experienced firsthand when you meditate. Let's say you sit quietly and observe your thoughts meditatively, i.e., you reflect on them. This would mean you are spending part of your attentiveness on shedding some light on your thoughts, but you also spend part of it on being the observer and interpreter of those thoughts. As such, you are connecting to your thoughts while keeping a certain level of detachment from them. We call this "connected but unattached." By this definition, you stop being meditative when you lose yourself in the object of your attention.

A Short History of Meditation

Indian wall art artifacts dating as far back as 5000 BCE show people seated in meditative postures. [18] Not that a posture defines meditation – you can sit cross-legged with your eyes closed and wish the worst on yourself and others. Early descriptions of meditations in the Indian Vedas, [19] originating around 1200 BCE, associate specific postures with practices of self-transformation. Interestingly, the descriptions in the Vedas also indicate that the earliest meditative practices often focused on objects, so the idea of meditation as a reflection process fits early practices.

Over time, many types of meditation evolved. Some had different objects of focus, such as expressions (mantras), cognitive and emotional constructs (like gratitude or happiness), one's passing thoughts or emotions (monitoring inner processes), imagined sensations (primarily visual or emotional), or external objects (like mandalas or things in nature). In recent years, various scientists have tried to define and categorize meditation based on these differences. [20] Open monitoring versus attention regulation is a common categorization based on the method of meditation. [21]

In open monitoring, attention is left free to focus on any object, i.e., it is not directed consciously. For example, as you meditate, you can give your attention the freedom to go toward your thoughts, how you feel, what you smell, or what you see without trying to be attentive to anything specific. This simple act of free attentiveness can bring your mind to a calm state. It turns out the awareness of your attention is calming, even if your attention itself is moving around.

The other category, attention regulation, uses a specific focus (or object of focus), and when attention drifts away from that object, an effort is made to bring it back there. A typical implementation of this is breath awareness meditation: you direct your attention to your breath, and when you become aware that your attention moves away from it (maybe to a thought), you consciously bring it back to your breath.

Although the open monitoring versus attention regulation categorization is not perfect, it is good enough to classify approaches such as Transcendental Meditation, Mindfulness Meditation, Loving-Kindness Meditation, Zazen, and Kriya Meditation as either leaning more toward open monitoring or attention regulation. The classification is also helpful for thinking about building progressing meditations: you should develop your awareness of your attention before moving to techniques to control it.

In War and Peace

The rise of the warrior elite (also called Bushi or Samurai) in feudal Japan coincided with the spread of Zen Buddhism in Asia. When Samurai prepared for battle, a great deal of thought went into strategy and tactics. At the same time, they were also aware of how thoughts and emotions could cloud the execution of those strategies when their actions needed to be swift and decisive. Therefore, a standard preparation for battle would not only involve making plans but also meditative quieting of the mind, commonly referred to as mokusō (黙想).

Figure 4. Samurai engaged in mokusō

The code by which the Samurai lived and fought (Bushido, the way of warriors) greatly emphasized cultivating a calm but alert state of mind that would be unclouded by emotions and detached from worldly desires. It was thought that this so-called unfettered mind was crucial to ensuring one could be at the right place at the right time on the battlefield. [22] To this day, the emphasis on meditation distinguishes traditional Japanese martial arts from most modern fight sports.

Meditation or Meditative?

Meditation has become a popular topic in blogs, newspaper articles, and podcasts, and more Western people are meditating than ever before. However, examining whether this meditation is truly a meditative practice is worth exploring.

Like yoga, meditation has come to be seen as an activity you do for a small period of your day. When done in groups, it is usually with like-minded people, making it easier and fun. Although these group meditations may be conducive to commercial implementation, it is far from certain that such practices translate to life. The question is not if you can meditate in a yoga studio but if you can be meditative in everyday life.

To understand the difference between meditating and being meditative, it is helpful to think of meditation as a training activity that is an investment for later. When you are meditative, you benefit from the return on that investment. The more functional you can make your meditations, the easier it becomes to be meditative. If your meditation is solely esoteric and unrelated to life, you may meditate in the early morning and find yourself in a rage an hour later.

Functional Before Spiritual

From Yogic traditions to Buddhist practices, meditation has been used to achieve some transcendence of consciousness. That could be as simple as perceiving life in and around us in a slightly more vibrant way. Still, it is often equated with more esoteric objectives that go beyond time and place on this planet to what many refer to as enlightenment. In mystic Indian traditions, this process is typically led by a guru. Interestingly, in one of the Upanishads, the word guru is explained as "someone who dispels darkness."[23] In that sense, a guru is simply someone carrying an extra torch and using it to light their path and that of others.

Unfortunately, the typical approach to meditation, guided by gurus or meditation apps, tends to be highly comfortable, spiritual, or both. We have already seen that comfort doesn't cultivate function, but going to a spiritual realm before taking care of basic functioning may seem attractive as a shortcut to a blissful life. Still, it cultivates a spirituality that misses impact (and meditation instructors who exhibit road rage when driving off the parking lot after their sessions). Our approach in this book addresses meditation and being meditative with a basics-to-function methodology, very similar to physical fitness training. Once you take care of the basics, you are in an excellent spot to go on a spiritual journey, although that is beyond the scope of this present book.

Functional Meditation

Functional meditation refers to a systematic approach to meditative exercise progressions that target the practical use of mental skills in life. This is very much like the training for functional physical fitness. For example, if you like hiking, you could work out to ensure you can do a challenging hike without getting tired. Or if you are a tennis player, you can work out to get faster on the court. This differs from working out to feel good or for aesthetic purposes. Applying this principle to meditation means designing your meditations to address a specific meditative activity in your day. For example, suppose you would like to give a presentation in a meditative flow of passion and excitement. You might use the days leading up to the presentation to do a series of meditations that progress from basic to something that is functionally very close to the actual presentation. Again, this is not so different from functional physical fitness training.

Functional meditation and mental fitness training both boil down to creating a balance between executing optimally in the moment (act in flow) on the one hand and using the past to plan for the future (reflect to grow) on the other hand. We'll take a good look at this duality in the next chapter.

> **Quick summary.** Meditation that does not lead to meditative experiences when it matters – in moments of pressure where the next action is critical – has no functional impact. While spiritual experiences may carry a lot of individual meaning, it can be argued that you should learn to walk before you run: learn to be functional in this life before you move beyond.

Meditation in focus. The meditative exercises introduced in this book optimize the way the mind interacts with the body. However, traditional forms of meditation, as they evolved from mysticism, were designed for a higher purpose: spiritual development. Some of the earliest descriptions of such practices are found in Indian texts called the Vedas, which have inspired many Indian philosophies, including Hinduism, Jainism, and Yogic traditions.

Although meditative methods and spiritual practices have evolved in various ways from their descriptions in the Vedas, a common thread in what was described in these texts and what we still see today is the attempt to initiate and cultivate a certain level of unity between the self and a higher reality. What is regarded as self and what is seen as higher reality depends on the school of thought.

Yoga is perhaps the most well-known approach towards spiritual development, although, for many, it has become a once-a-week stretch and sweat session led by someone with flexible limbs. Originally, however, yoga was a practical methodology to work towards a more enlightened self. [24] Self, in Yogic traditions, has different layers, some more basic and physical, others more complex and spiritual.

The systematic methodology introduced in this book concerns itself only with the physical (your body as an accumulation of nutrients), physiological (your body as an energy transference system), and mental layers (your body as an information processing system). The fact that we don't go beyond managing these basic three does not mean that the skills you develop cannot be a solid foundation for a deeper journey. It is just that in this book, we chose to cover the basics first.

Chapter 5

A TALE OF TWO MINDS

"Our ability to reflect has brought us to the top of the food chain. It hasn't helped us much with enjoying the food."

The Nature of Attention

To understand how we perceive and operate the various states of our mind, it's essential first to understand attention. The nature of attention is often compared to a flashlight. It can not only be pointed at something or move around at different speeds and frequencies, but it also has different beams: narrow or wide, bright or dim. However, while this may clarify attention, it does not do full justice to the broader idea of attentiveness.

While attention is something you give, attentiveness is something you have. It requires not only directed attention but also a processing of information. The flashlight metaphor no longer works for attentiveness, but a good alternative is a high-end camera.

Like a flashlight, a camera can be pointed at something, and it can move around at different speeds. Beyond the direction of the camera, the lenses (wide-angle, high-zoom, or macro) also determine how space is captured. So far, the flashlight and camera analogies are very similar, but the camera analogy can go further. It can extract information from an observed scene in different ways. Some lenses let more light through than others, but more importantly, aperture, shutter speed, and ISO settings can render completely different pictures. And if you think of attentiveness as a semi-continuous stream, imagine you are recording videos rather than pictures.

This brings up an interesting thing about how our brain generates attentiveness. It turns out we perceive our environment not in a continuous stream but in bursts of attentiveness that range from four to ten pulses a second (4-10 Hz). [25] Our seemingly continuous notion of reality is, therefore, an illusion – our brain fills in the gaps. This rhythmic nature of our attention nevertheless provides a physiological foundation of why certain people can feel time slowing down when they are in a state of flow. For example, professional athletes may be able to bring their attention rhythm to a higher frequency while keeping the same density of perception (i.e., increasing the framerate of their camera while keeping all other settings the same). This allows them to effectively process more information within the same timeframe, making it easier to distinguish details and perceive a slowing down of time. [26]

Awareness

Attention can be used to shine a light on many things. When you use it to attend to the inner workings of your mind, we refer to it as self-attention or awareness.

As soon as awareness comes into play, it becomes evident that we have two distinctively different states of mind. The reason for this is that our self-attention is notoriously bad at multitasking if the observed mental activities are either reflection-driven or perception-driven. The challenge for our attention is caused by the fact that the neurophysiology of reflection and its consequences is very different from the neurophysiology of perception and its consequences.

For example, reflections rely heavily on stored information in advanced areas of our brain. Think of thoughts running through your mind, the emotions that may be associated with the thoughts, and then subsequent thoughts that are provoked by the emotions. Unsurprisingly, the processing frequencies of the brain waves that are present while reflecting tend to be very high.

Perceptions, on the other hand, rely more on peripheral sensory systems and phylogenetically lower (more basic) parts of our brain to process information from the present and (re)act. Think jumping on a trampoline and sensing your balance while you're in the air, feeling the power of the trampoline propel you up, and repeating that to stay upright for a number of jumps. The brain waves involved in that can peak but are, on average, much lower in frequency than when the activity is reflection-driven, and they spike in different parts of the brain.

Because these activities involve our brain and nervous system in different ways and with different urgency, our attention tends to get absorbed by one of the two, not both at the same time. For example, when your attention is deeply engaged with thoughts or emotions rooted in the past or future, it's tough to be attentive to what your senses are bringing you from the present. Similarly, when your senses absorb your attention, it's tough to think clearly about the past or present. This is why awareness and awareness training is so important: if you can keep a small part of your attentive energy for self-attention, you can be aware of the state of mind that your attention is drawn to (and is most active). This, then, allows you not to get lost in either state of mind unless you want to. It gives you the ability to think deeply but not get lost in thoughts. To be intensely passionate but not ruled by emotions. Or be fully in the moment but with the option to step out of it.

Mind State Versus Mindset

In this book, we explicitly distinguish a state of mind from a mindset. The topic of mindsets was brought to mainstream psychology by Carol Dweck [27] and is extensively covered in psychology and self-help literature. A mindset is a conviction about personal characteristics and abilities, and typically, a distinction is made between people who tend to view their abilities as relatively static (fixed mindset) or relatively evolving (a growth mindset). Although this is a valuable categorization and helps move someone from a fixed mindset to a growth mindset and can change their attitude towards life, it does not go beyond that – an attitude. In other words, you can have a growth mindset, but you may still be unable to make meaningful changes to your behavior because you don't have the skills.

A state of mind is not based on an attitude or conviction but on a physiological state of the central nervous system. We have already seen that, based on the limits of attention, we can distinguish a state in which the brain prioritizes reflection (engaged in the past or future) or action (engaged in the present experience). It's time to take a deeper look at these mind states.

Contemplative Versus Operative

A contemplative state is a state in which we evaluate moments from the past or anticipate moments in the future. The purpose of this is to learn and grow, and it involves three powerful modalities: thoughts, projections, and emotions. Thinking about the past and future is essential for survival. Projections (imaginations, dreams, and visions) help us shape a future that sets out a path for our well-being. Meanwhile, emotions, when used positively, are powerful motivators of behavior. However, whatever the nature of the contemplation and no matter how useful, it distracts, by very definition, from our sensory perception of the reality at hand.

In an operative state, we are engaged in the present moment, at a current place, and in full awareness of our perceptions. Our mind is not reflecting to learn and grow, but it is driven by perceptions, to act and flow. Being in the moment means we are connected but not attached or tethered to something; attachment will immediately disrupt the flow. This is because of the nature of a moment: it lasts only, well, a moment, and the instant you linger in it, you are, in fact, in the past.

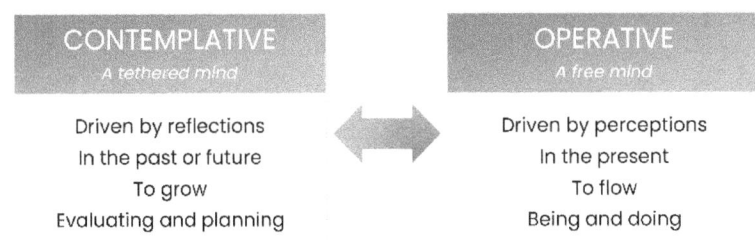

Figure 5. The two states of mind

Neither mind state is inherently good or bad. What matters is the time and place you use them. Sports activities are great to illustrate that. For example, before a soccer match, a team should discuss the strategy and tactics, and that requires being contemplative. Ideally, everyone on the team should use visualization techniques to imprint various strategic scenarios in their brain. By the way, Pele was famous for doing that. [28] However, the moment soccer players make a pass or are in the middle of taking a penalty kick, their minds should be wholly operative and in the moment. The same is true for golfers walking up to the tee. There should be a plan and a vision of the plan, but at the moment of executing the swing, their mind should be free and in the present.

A Monkey Mind

The terms monkey mind and mind monkey are commonly used in Buddhist publications to refer to the distracting or anxious chatter of your inner dialogue. [29] The monkey, so to speak, is out of control and doesn't stop telling you things you don't want to hear. The concept and metaphor are very relatable – who doesn't have a mind monkey now and then – and it has been adopted and depicted in graphic art, poetry, theater, and literature for centuries. A monkey mind, however, is not quite the same as our contemplative state of mind, and it is worth clarifying the differences.

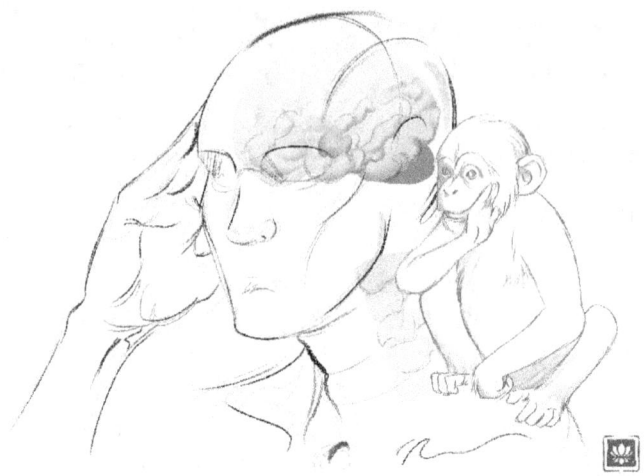

Figure 6. A monkey mind

Mind monkeys are usually depicted as disturbers of the peace. In other words, they bring racing thoughts and negative emotions such as doubt, anxiety, restlessness, and even fear and anger. While our contemplative state of mind can do all that, it is also capable of many positive contemplative things. For example, weighing the positives and negatives of a decision is a prudent thing to do and can be done positively, in complete control over your thoughts. Contemplating positively on things in your imagination can motivate positive actions. Nothing is out of control in your brain when you do these things.

So, while every mind monkey is a contemplation, taking you out of the present into negativity, not every contemplation is a mind monkey. Contemplations can be creative and positive. In fact, from an evolutionary perspective, it is partly what brought humans to the top of the food chain. The challenge is when to contemplate and when to operate. You don't want to be contemplative when a mountain lion attacks you, but you do when you survive the attack and want to plan a course of action to prevent such an attack from ever happening again. Similarly, you do want to be operative when you enjoy good food or enjoy cooking it, but you'd better be contemplative when you create your grocery list and plan your shopping.

Quick summary. Mental fitness depends on our ability to reflect and act appropriately, at the right moment and in the right place. Reflecting is done with a contemplative state of mind and involves the past and future. Acting requires an operative state of mind, present in the moment and driven by perceptions of the situation at hand. Both activities can be done mindfully.

🪷 Two minds in perspective. There are a number of concepts that resemble the operative and contemplative mind states. The most common associations are mindfulness versus mindlessness and Timothy Gallwey's Self 1 and Self 2. [30]

First of all, one may (wrongfully) think that mindfulness is the same as being in an operative state of mind. However, the Pali term from which mindfulness is derived, Sati, refers to "an awareness of things in relation to things, and hence an awareness of their relative value." [31] Hence, mindfulness is about presence in perspective, not just an awareness that is driven by perceptions. While mindfulness can be operative (perceiving and acting in the present moment), it can also be contemplative (observing thoughts or emotions).

In the 80s and 90s, Timothy Gallwey published a number "Inner Game" books that were influential in sports such as tennis and golf. The Inner Game approach describes Self 1 as "the conscious ego mind that we as humans have invented on top of the real self that we were born with" and Self 2 as "the human being itself." Self 1 is seen as interference: "It is like a damaged floppy disk giving orders to a billion-dollar mainframe." Subsequently, the idea is to take Self 1 out of the equation. Hence, Self 1 and 2 are very different from contemplative and operative states, respectively. Being contemplative or operative is neither good nor bad; it is simply about different brain patterns. Our brain is capable of these patterns because there is a utility to them, and whether one or the other should be more active will depend on the circumstances.

In summary, the two states of mind laid out in this book refer to neurophysiological states. As such, they are fundamentally different from constructs that describe activities or entities, like mindfulness or Self 1 and Self 2.

Chapter 6

MIND MANAGEMENT

*"At any moment of action,
all there is... is the moment!
No past, no future, just now."*

Managing Mind States

Now that we have established that our brain fluctuates between predominantly contemplative (processing thoughts and emotions concerning past or future moments, other places) and predominantly operative (processing observations and actions in the moment, right here), the logical next question is: "Can we develop an ability to control these mind states? And can we manage them so we can use them optimally when they are needed?" The answer is a resounding "yes".

There is no good or bad when it comes to contemplative and operative mind states, but there are undoubtedly wrong times and places for each. In other words, the question becomes, "When do we use which?" As a basic rule, if there is no direct threat or challenge, there is an opportunity for evaluating and planning without the danger of being hurt. This is the ultimate time to be contemplative. On the other hand, if there is a direct threat or challenge, it is time to trust what you learned and trained and just do it! Hence, this is the time to be operative and flow. While these are typical scenarios and rules of thumb, there are many situations in which you need a bit of both. You may have to calm your mind, evaluate the situation, and plan in a matter of seconds, and then go operative again. Recognizing these situations and adjusting your state of mind for optimal behavior can be referred to as mind management.

Following the suggestions in our Flow Series books (or the online platform), you will learn about training methods to develop and maintain contemplative and operative skills. This is not so different from how the samurai did it, except explicitly structured. In addition, you will adopt relevant perspectives and cultivate positive emotions for use in pressure situations. To keep things simple, we have selected five core skills and five core perspectives common in meditative practices and peak performance assessments and will focus on those only.

Five Core Skills

There are five critical mental skills that correspond to stages in meditative practices. They can also be seen in peak performers' preparation, performance, and recovery routines, and they even come back as steps in clinical hypnotherapy sessions (see the insight box at the end of the chapter). They have a logical order, and with a bit of creativity, these five skills can be described by five words that start with the letter R. All these skills are on a spectrum between completely operative and contemplative.

Realize – Realizing, in the context of our five core mental skills, is not about coming to a logical conclusion. It is about seeing reality as it is. The first prerequisite for this is a calm or quiet mind. If your state of mind is not calm (for example, with racing thoughts or emotions), your perception of reality is clouded. A common analogy is that of a mental lake that reflects reality. If you don't keep the lake calm, the ripples and waves will distort reality. Training realization as a skill starts with internal awareness exercises that cover attention, such as attention awareness, attention control, attentive breathing, and attentive tension regulation. You may recognize some of these as mindfulness techniques, except we structure them based on training principles (covered in the next chapter). The realization techniques help you reduce the activity of your conscious mind and perceive with a certain level of connected detachment. The start of mental exercise flows and routines is always a calm mind.

Relax – Relaxing is mainly about the downregulation of the base tension of our body. This relates to your heart rate, blood pressure, muscle tension, sweating, digestive activity, and even clarity of thinking. Training this skill involves physical techniques (such as breath and movement control) and suggestive techniques (such as projections).

Reason – Reasoning is about effective analysis and decision-making, especially as you are aware of it with an inner dialogue. Reasoning is easily overdone and is where many people find themselves lost. Training standardized inner dialogue structures to describe, decide, and affirm can help tremendously with the ability to create reason in what may appear as chaos under stress.

Revise – Revising is about correcting and directing behavior. Since behavior is primarily subconscious, it is essential to reach that part of our mind when making behavioral changes. More so than verbal suggestions, projections of imagined corrective experiences that involve all senses (and even emotional aspects) are the most potent agents of change.

Refocus – In the end, you must prepare to go from being to doing. At the moment of execution, there is no time for a calming exercise, a relaxing breath, an inner dialogue, or even a visualization. At any moment of action, all there is... is the moment! No past, no future, just now. This requires you to be all in - fully present - and external awareness exercises are at the core of optimal interactions with your environment.

SKILL	ACTIVITY
Realize	Calming your mind
Relax	Reducing tension
Reason	Optimizing thoughts
Revise	Correcting behavior
Refocus	Engaging your mind

Table 1. The five core mental skills

The order of the skills is based on how they are used in meditative practices and behavioral therapy sessions: (1) with a calm mind to see reality, your relaxation techniques work optimally; (2) with good relaxation, you will be able to reason with clear thoughts, (3) with clear thinking you can make a plan for correcting your behavior; (4) imagining and projecting changes in your mind makes it easier for your body to follow, and (5) with all these preparations in place, you can refocus and let it happen.

Five Core Perspectives and Emotions

A perspective is a belief or conviction. It is not just a thought but something more permanent that drives behavioral patterns. A perspective is a cognitive psychological attribute, and it has an associated emotional attribute. If the perspective is positive, the emotional association is also positive – a positive emotion. For example, the perspective that life is a gift can generate a feeling of joy and lightheartedness.

On the other hand, if the perspective is negative, the associated emotion is also negative. The perspective that you are a failure at something can generate a feeling of inadequacy and sadness. The strength of the connection between perspectives and their associated emotions is personal and can be cultivated by training.

There are five core perspectives, and they have their origin in the most common positive emotions that are triggered in meditative practices. It is not a coincidence that emotions such as gratitude, joyfulness, passion, compassion, and kindness are seen as vehicles of transformation in meditative practices that originated independently across continents and cultures. These emotions were identified as essential to individual and community health.

Gift – The first and perhaps most fundamental perspective for overall well-being is the conviction that every moment you experience is a gift in itself. You realize that the gift may not be apparent at the time, but you are convinced it is there for you to discover. While this perspective is mainly associated with the positive emotion of gratitude, other positive emotions follow from here naturally. For example, a deeply felt gratitude can generate happiness, passion, excitement, and kindness.

Celebration – From a celebration perspective, every moment in life has a seed of joy. It's like life is a festival, and while there may be unfortunate moments in that festival as well, it is meant to be experienced with a light heart. Of all the life forms on this planet, only human beings take themselves so seriously that they turn their mental energy into misery. While you have no control over many external situations that cause pain, whether you let these situations create a negative spiral depends on your control over your mental faculties and your ability to keep a light heart.

Opportunity – Every experience is an opportunity to use your energy for something unique. In Japanese, there is a saying, "ichi go ichi e" (一期一会), which tells you that every meeting is a unique chance. [32] It's like "carpe diem," but with the energy to seize every day as if it is a first experience rather than your last. With this perspective, even mundane tasks can become something to be excited and passionate about. Commitment, determination, and dedication are all mental attributes that follow from this perspective.

Lesson – When you see that you can learn from every experience, no matter the outcome, you realize that every moment deserves an engaged, open mind. Curiosity comes effortlessly, and value comes from the lesson itself, not where it takes you. In addition, when outcomes become secondary – almost like a side effect – this creates emotional stability and calmness. Even confidence is related to this perspective, albeit not based on achieving results but on the conviction that results will follow where lessons are learned. It's important to understand that this differs greatly from not being interested in results. In the end, results do matter, and survival matters, but worrying about results doesn't help performance.

Connection – The last perspective brings it all together. It is the perspective that life is a connecting journey. When you stop identifying yourself with all things that set you apart and start identifying with all things that connect, you can be right where you need to be – always. Experiences, even tough ones, can become fulfilling and meaningful when boundaries between what you experience as internal and external fade. You will belong and contribute to a belonging environment with sincere kindness.

If you study the perspectives and positive emotions carefully, you can see that one emotion can lead to another. Just like there is an order in core skills, there is also an order in core perspectives and core positive emotions. Ultimately, they generate a mix of emotions that reinforce each other, like a virtuous cycle or positive spiral. While attributes must be trained, they are trained differently than skills: skills are trained directly with specific techniques, whereas perspectives are cultivated indirectly in training by keeping them stable in challenging conditions.

PERSPECTIVES	EMOTIONS
Gift	Gratitude, thankfulness, appreciation
Celebration	Joy, happiness, lightheartedness
Opportunity	Passion, motivation, determination
Lesson	Curiosity, open-mindedness, stability
Connection	Belonging, kindness, freedom

Table 2. The five core perspectives and associated emotions

Flow 255®

Flow 255® is an online mental fitness platform that was developed by 2Mynds based on the theory outlined in this book. It is named after the two states of mind, five skills, and five perspectives, and it combines the 2-5-5 methodology with exercise physiology and gamified platform technology to create a mental training tool that helps you train your mind like you train your body.

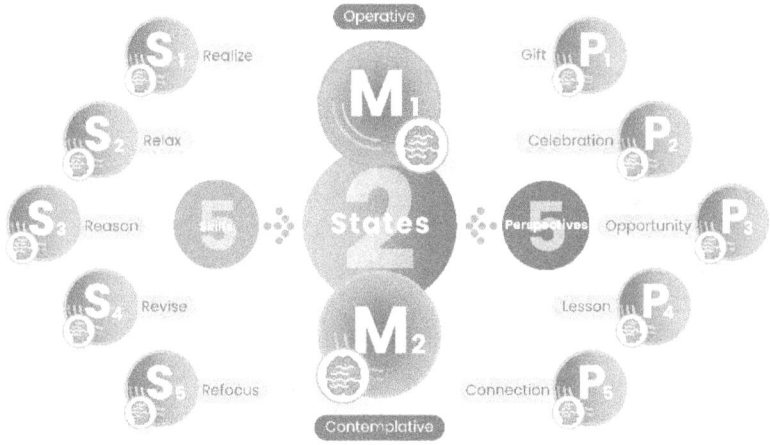

Figure 7. The Flow 255 method

The training platform is like an online mental fitness gym, with a dashboard, assessments, training library, guided meditation audio clips, and application videos that help integrate mental skills into performance situations. Personalization is available via daily flow suggestions, and unique playlists keep everyone on track and accountable.

Lastly, as a training tool, Flow 255® is not just for individuals but also has dedicated features for teams and managing teams. This makes it a unique add-on for psychologists, performance coaches, and human resource departments who manage clients and teams that perform critical activities under pressure. You can find the platform and more at www.2mynds.com.

Toward Change

While skills are to be trained, psychological attributes such as perspectives and emotional tendencies have some level of hereditary origin and trait-like character [33]. While the genetic foundation on which these attributes develop is beyond our control, brain patterns associated with perspectives and emotional control are sensitive to influence from parents, peers, society, and, last but not least, training. The next chapter will define a stepwise methodology for making the training for mental fitness effective, and the next book in this series will cover the relevant exercise physiology, as well as a progressive overview of techniques, exercises, and workout periodizations.

Quick summary. Controlling our contemplative and operative states requires specific core mental skills and perspectives. All perspectives are associated with specific positive emotions This book proposes five core skills and five core perspectives. The skills can be trained directly in exercises and workouts, whereas perspectives must be cultivated indirectly in training.

A link to hypnotherapy. The five primary mental skills proposed in this book come from a careful assessment of common steps in meditative practices. However, there is an interesting resemblance between the five primary mental skills and typical parts of a clinical hypnotherapy session. Most forms of hypnotherapy (traditional, Ericksonian, solution-focused, cognitive-behavioral) will follow this sequence:

1. Inducting: Initiate a calm mind and relaxed body
2. Deepening: Deep relaxation; access subconscious
3. Instructing: Correct patterns via logical directions
4. Suggesting: Correct patterns via projections
5. Emerging: Come back to conscious awareness

Depending on the type of hypnotherapy, there may be an emphasis on particular steps, or they may be combined. These steps line up almost seamlessly with the five primary mental skills - even the order is identical: (1) realize > induction, (2) relax > deepening, (3) reason > instructing, (4) revise > suggesting, (5) refocus > emerging.

Although the methodology for mental fitness outlined in the Flow Series books is not based on any form of hypnotherapy, the resemblance of the core mental skills to the hypnotherapy steps comes as no surprise. After all, many meditative practices could be considered a form of gentle self-hypnosis. One significant difference between mental fitness training and hypnotherapy to keep in mind is that mental fitness training should be used as a preventative activity and not as a therapeutic one.

Chapter 7

ONE STEP AT A TIME

*"Our mind and body are connected
from the day we are born until the day
we die; why train them separately?"*

The Development Cycle

The process of developing fitness, mental or physical, has no beginning and no end. At any apparent start, you are building on what you already have. And when you think you are done, you are at the beginning of the next iteration. To make this cyclical process functional, your development will need at least these three steps: (1) assess, (2) acquire, and (3) apply. Each step has core activities.

STEP	ACTIVITY
Assess	Test, track
Acquire	Learn, train
Apply	Transfer, integrate

Table 3. The three steps of a fitness development cycle

A proper development cycle starts with testing and preparing your stats so you can track your progress (assess). Next, you learn and train to develop skills and attributes (acquire). Finally, you transfer everything you learned and trained to functional situations before you integrate it into activities that matter (apply). As you apply, you will likely become aware of strengths and deficiencies and will confirm that when you retest, which marks the repetition point of the cycle. Let's look at how each step applies to mental fitness.

Assessing Mental Fitness

Assessing mental fitness is done in two steps: first, you test, and then you track. Testing in mental health can be referred to as mental measurements or psychometrics. These tests target specific psychological attributes or skills. Traditionally, the measurements are made through self-reported questionnaires, but the technology to measure physiological properties – biometrics - related to our psychology is becoming increasingly sophisticated.

While self-reported psychometrics have the disadvantage of being subjective and dependent on a person's insight and honesty, they have the advantage that they can explicitly target specific skills and attributes. So, you can ask people about focus, relaxation, or mood. Biometrics, on the other hand, while objectively measured, only detect consequences of mental capacities and processes. Some are more related to the constructs they are meant to measure than others, but this is hard to quantify; the associations between the metric and the target construct are often weak, and the measurements tend to be relatively imprecise.

Besides assessing fitness aspects, exploring and defining targets and goals based on those aspects is also important. Your short-term targets are typically based on the test results, and the long-term goals can have their roots in your motivations. Both are instrumental in guiding your learning and training steps.

Another critical component of mental fitness assessments is tracking results over time. This requires summary statistics, analytics, and visualization. Scores can be categorized by domain (like specific skills or attributes), averaged, and plotted over time. Also, biometrics lend themselves well to analysis and visualization because they tend to be quantitative. Psychometrics are inherently more qualitative, so often, a scoring algorithm is needed to generate meaningful statistics.

As a side note, mental fitness should always be quantified in reference to overall mental health and living conditions. So, a good mental fitness assessment includes an assessment of physical health and the main domains of general mental health. While mental fitness can affect mental and physical health, the presence or absence of disorders also impacts which mental training methods can be used and how they will impact mental fitness.

Acquiring Mental Fitness

The most significant step in developing mental fitness is the acquisition of skills and attributes (perspectives and emotional control). This involves both learning and training. Learning is about cognitive development and gaining knowledge. For many, developing an understanding is a critical element of acquiring skills, but its importance depends on personal preferences and inclinations. Consider someone learning how to throw an American football. Most people will appreciate some verbal explanation on how to hold the ball, take the throwing arm back, accelerate your arm, and use your body to throw the ball. However, some will develop more quickly when they can start by throwing the ball and exploring the experience with only minimal information. This is called explicit and implicit learning, respectfully. There is no right or wrong, although generally, a small amount of knowledge development should precede an exercise.

Learning mental skills itself can happen in many ways. For example, you are reading this book, which should make you more knowledgeable about mental fitness and flow. However, if you would talk to me in person and could ask me questions, you'd have a different, probably better, learning experience. Similarly, if I conveyed this information in a prerecorded interview video, you might pick up yet other things. Nowadays, a well-designed e-learning system can combine the above and add an interactive component to optimize the transfer of information.

Training mental skills, however, always involves exercises that take you beyond what you know. In training, you challenge your skill level in an exercise routine, repeat it until it becomes easier, and then progress to more challenging exercises. To do this efficiently and to address different functional components, exercises must be combined in workouts, and workouts must be combined in workout plans. This is how it works for physical fitness, and it applies equally to mental fitness. Since your brain is a physical organ, it reacts to a training stimulus the same way as any other organ in your body: only a stimulus that disrupts a specific part of an individual repeatedly, with a frequency, intensity, functionality, and type that progresses, will result in the compensation and adaptation that prevents functional failure of that part in the future.

The description above references the core training principles from exercise physiology and sports science. Unfortunately, to the date of this writing, these training principles are rarely applied to preventative interventions for mental health (mental fitness training). The key reason for writing this book series and developing the Flow 255® online mental fitness system is to facilitate that change.

Applying Mental Fitness

Transferring your knowledge and skills to situations and moments when they count most also requires practice. After all, when there is a lot at stake (or it seems that way), chances are that your skills and perspectives somehow don't feel at home. The solution is to start with the least stressful life situations and then progress the transfer to more challenging and performative circumstances in sports, music, school, or work.

For example, suppose you are a professional tennis player, and you have acquired mental skills to a basic level and have only applied the techniques in routines during practice, never in a tournament. In that case, you would not expect these skills to work flawlessly when you start applying them in a match at Wimbledon. The gap would be too big. You would not make that mistake for applications of your physical fitness, so don't make it for applications of mental fitness!

When applying mental skills, you might first incorporate the techniques in morning and evening routines, pre- and post-match routines before training, practice matches, and then all of the above on-site at Wimbledon. While doing this, you may increase stress triggers around your routines and make your techniques and routines more stress-resistant.

The best way to develop solid routines is to use a similar structure across routines. In the Flow 255® approach, the five core mental skills become the core components of all routines. This way, routines that transfer skills to low-stress daily life will help the routines that integrate skills in competitive performance situations. This standardized approach to routines makes it easier for your brain to develop stable patterns that are resilient to pressure.

From Cycle to Spiral

The assess-acquire-apply cycle is crucial for developing mental fitness, but repeating the same cycle at the same intensity over and over will only take you to a certain point, and you will not develop beyond. Most certainly, your fitness will not become stress-resistant. To develop mental fitness to functional levels, the cycles must progress. In terms well-known in exercise physiology and physical training methodology, there must be a progressive overload that is challenging but not inhibiting or compromising. In simpler terms, the spiral should progress to a level of stress that is functional. For example, an athlete should assess, acquire, and apply mental skills under stress progressions that build up over time until the physiology during the cycle is similar to the physiology that is experienced in competition. Without these progressive spirals, mental techniques won't work when it matters.

Many different modalities can be used to progress the spiral. Virtually any exposure that disrupts the status quo of our mind-body complex can create an overload progression: cold, heat, lack of food, lack of sleep, lack of oxygen, fear, and even excitement. However, one stands out regarding ease of regulation, accessibility, and applicability: physical exercise. The next book in this series covers the methodology to use progressive overload from physical exercise in mental fitness training in great detail. Meanwhile, a quick summary is given below, and you can use the online Flow 255® platform by 2Mynds to put everything into practice.

Any physical exercise taken to failure will generate an acute stress response, and the stress response is, generally speaking, proportional to the level of failure. When exercising, failure is most easily accomplished and regulated if it affects muscular strength, muscular endurance, cardiorespiratory endurance, or a combination. By designing physical exercise flows that specifically address one or more of these components, we can have sections in our mental fitness workouts that have the purpose of providing controlled levels of acute stress. Combining these sections with mental exercise flow sections allows us to create periodized mind-body flow workouts that progress the spiral.

Finally, the training principles of progression and overload also apply to mental exercise flows: within and across workouts, mental exercises should gradually get more challenging. This is laid out in detail in the next book in this series, and it forms the backbone of the workout playlists in the Flow 255® platform.

Next Steps

This chapter concludes the description of an innovative theoretical framework for mental fitness training. The framework aims to shift the paradigm of mental health and performance interventions - from insights to skills, support to training, and therapy to prevention. The proposed paradigm shift does not ignore or downplay the importance of support and therapy. Still, it does give mental fitness training based on exercise physiology a more prominent role.

This book is meant to inspire and inform; by itself, it can never be the driver of change – that can only be you. If you enjoy reading about how to train, the next book in this Flow Series will suggest an abundance of techniques, exercises, and workouts to achieve and maintain mental fitness. However, if you are looking to get your reps in for your mental fitness and train your mind like you train your body, the Flow 255® platform is the tool you are looking for.

In conclusion, mental fitness is not developed through knowledge but through training. That mental training is not a one-and-done activity but a journey with ups and downs. A journey on which you just took a nice big step forward.

Quick summary. Development cycles in physical and mental fitness training have three core steps in common: (1) assess, (2) acquire, and (3) apply. These steps are in their natural order and should be repeated in a positive spiral. The spiral's main underlying force is progressive overload: training should progress to stress. The online Flow 255® system by 2Mynds puts this approach into practice.

From training to applying. Training a skill is not the same as applying a skill. This is why carpenters go to school and do assignments on the job before they take responsibility for large projects. It is why professional athletes do not just compete but spend at least an hour or more in the gym every day and transition the gym work to their competitive environment. Even though training and applying are distinctly different, it is not a dichotomy but a spectrum with gradual transitions.

On the training end of the spectrum is an activity that reflects an investment for the future. There is no immediate performance improvement at the moment of training or directly after. In fact, if a workout follows training principles of exercise physiology, systems are overloaded to failure and are fatigued, leading to reduced performance directly after training. However, the investment lies in the adaptation response that follows and an over-compensation that leads to increased performance.

On the applying end of the spectrum is an activity that uses techniques from training and integrates them fully into performance with the immediate purpose of improving that performance. As such, applying always takes place at a performative place and time. For athletes, that means they apply as they compete. There are, however, steps in between that progress from fundamental training to functional training to competitive integration, as illustrated in the graphic below.

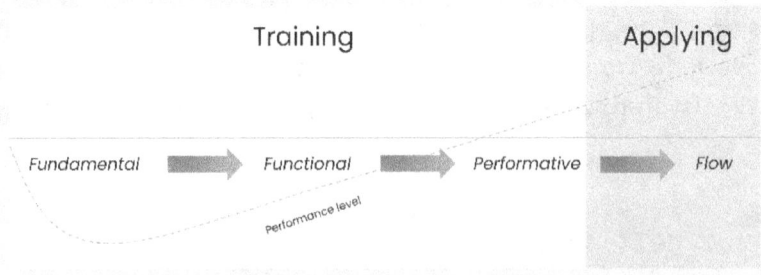

Figure 8. From training to applying

BIBLIOGRAPHY

1. 2Mynds, Inc, "2Mynds. Mental Fitness Training to Unleash Your Mind," [Online]. Available: https://www.2Mynds.com. [Accessed 12 Sep 2023].

2. B. Jowett, "Plato, The Apology of Socrates, 21d," The Center for Hellenic Studies, Harvard, Boston, 2020.

3. Wikipedia, "Analysis paralysis," [Online]. Available: https://en.wikipedia.org/wiki/Analysis_paralysis. [Accessed 12 Sep 2023].

4. E. L. Johnson, J. W. Y. Kam, A. Tsovara and R. T. Knight, "Insights into human cognition from intracranial EEG: A review of audition, memory, internal cognition, and causality," *Journal of Neural Engineering,* vol. 17, no. 5, p. 051001, 2020.

5. D. Lorenz and S. Morrison, "Current Concepts in Periodization of Strength and Conditioning for the Sports Physical therapist," *International Journal of Sports Physical Therapy ,* vol. 10, no. 6, pp. 734-47, 2015.

6. Wikipedia, "Physical Fitness," [Online]. Available: https://en.wikipedia.org/wiki/Physical_fitness. [Accessed 12 Sep 2023].

7. S. Ries, N. Dronkers and R. Knight, "Choosing words: left hemisphere, right hemisphere, or both? Perspective on the lateralization of word retrieval," *Annals of the New York Academy of Sciences,* vol. 1369, no. 1, p. 111–131, 2016.

8. C. Sissons, "What is the Average Percentage of Water in the Human Body?," 27 May 2020. [Online]. Available: https://www.medicalnewstoday.com/articles/what-percentage-of-the-human-body-is-water. [Accessed 11 September 2023].

9. Wikipedia, "Fight-or-flight Response," [Online]. Available: https://en.wikipedia.org/wiki/Fight-or-flight_response. [Accessed 12 Sep 2023].

10. B. Chu, K. Marwaha, T. Sanvictores and D. Ayers, "Physiology, Stress Reaction," in *StatPearls*, Treasure Island (FL), StatPearls Publishing, 2022.

11. S. Hofmann, S. Heering, A. Sawyer and A. Asnaani, "How to handle anxiety: The effects of reappraisal, acceptance, and suppression strategies on anxious arousal," *Behaviour research and therapy,* vol. 47, no. 5, p. 389–394, 2009.

12. M. Csikszentmihalyi, Flow, New York: Harper & Row, 1990.

13. A. Maslow, Religions, values, and peak experiences, London: Penguin Books Limited, 1964.

14. F. Ashe and A. Deford, "Diary Entry February 18, 1974 (London WCT)," in *Arthur Ashe: Portrait in Motion*, Wilmington, MS, Houghton Mifflin, 1975, p. 272.

15. J. E. Loehr, The New Toughness Training for Sports, New York: Penguin Group, 1995.

16. Wikipedia, "Wu Wei," [Online]. Available: https://en.wikipedia.org/wiki/Wu_wei. [Accessed 9 Sep 2023].

17. M. Aurelius, Meditations, Gutenberg Project, 2001.

18. Wikipedia, "History of Meditation," [Online]. Available: https://en.wikipedia.org/wiki/History_of_meditation/. [Accessed 2023 Sep 2023].

19. Wikipedia, "Vedas," Wikipedia, [Online]. Available: https://en.wikipedia.org/wiki/Vedas. [Accessed 9 Sep 2023].

20. J. Nash, A. Newberg and B. Awasthi, "Toward a unifying taxonomy and definition for meditation," *Front Psychol,* vol. 4, pp. 1–14, 2013.

21. A. Lutz, H. Slagter, J. Dunne and R. Davidson, "Attention regulation and monitoring in meditation," *Trends Cogn Sci,* vol. 12, no. 4, pp. 163-169, 2008.

22. T. Soho, The Unfettered Mind; Writings from a Zen Master to a Master Swordsman, Boston: Shambala Publications, 2012.

23. M. Muller, The Upanishads (Advayataraka Upanishad, Verse 16), Oxford: Clarendon Press, 1879.

24. Sadhguru, "What Yoga Really Means," [Online]. Available: https://isha.sadhguru.org/yoga/yoga-articles-yoga/what-is-yoga/. [Accessed 12 Sep 2023].

25. R. F. Helfrich, I. C. Fiebelkorn, S. S. M, J. J. Lin and J. Parvizi, "Neural Mechanisms of Sustained Attention Are Rhythmic," *Neuron,* vol. 99, no. 4, pp. 854-865, 2018.

26. O. Sacks, "Speed; A Neurologist's Notebook," *The New Yorker,* vol. 8, no. 23, pp. 60-69, 2004.

27. C. S. Dweck, Mindset: The New Psychology Of Success, New York: Ballantine Books, 2007.

28. G. Plimpton, Sports!, Abradale Press, 1983.

29. Wikipedia, "Monkey Mind," [Online]. Available: https://en.wikipedia.org/wiki/Monkey_mind. [Accessed 25 Oct 2023].

30. Wikipedia, "Timothy Gallwey," [Online]. Available: https://en.wikipedia.org/wiki/. [Accessed 5 11 2023].

31. R. H. Sharf, "Mindfulness and Mindlessness in Early Chan," *Philosophy East and West,* vol. 64, pp. 933 - 964, 2014.

32. Wikipedia, "Ichi-go ichi-e," [Online]. Available: https://en.wikipedia.org/wiki/Ichi-go_ichi-e. [Accessed 24 October 2023].

33. S. Sanchez-Roige, J. Gray, J. MacKillop, C. Chen and A. Palmer, "The genetics of human personality," *Genes, Brain and Behavior,* vol. 17, no. 3, 2018.

INDEX

ABOUT THE AUTHOR

As a medical scientist, Leon worked on cutting-edge projects in academia and industry. His work focused on optimizing therapeutic interventions, initially as a research scientist and professor at medical school and later at biosimulation startups in Silicon Valley. In 2017, he decided he wanted to be more involved in the betterment of society and less in the betterment of pharmaceutical revenue streams. Through his work, he knew mental problems were highly prevalent, with generally poorly working therapeutics addressing them. More importantly, preventative interventions were virtually non-existent because they received little interest from the industry. He subsequently pulled together his scientific expertise in physical therapy, exercise science, clinical epidemiology, and medical informatics and a lifelong experience in meditation, martial arts, and high-performance competitive sports. His first order of business was creating a methodology for mental fitness training and scalable technology to test the method. A pilot project explored if principles from exercise physiology could be applied to sports psychology. The idea was to create mental training regimens based on the same training principles that were used for physical fitness. This resulted in a methodology called Flow 255®: mind-body training to optimally manage two states of mind with five skills and five perspectives. The system was initially tested by professional and nationally ranked junior tennis players, but the approach was soon expanded to other athletes and even beyond sports. Upon proving the concept, Leon founded 2Mynds, Inc., a hybrid social venture and tech startup with the mission to build a society where everyone can thrive at life, even under pressure.

 # ABOUT 2MYNDS

2Mynds was founded by Leon Bax. It was created as a combination of a mental fitness startup and social venture: innovative and agile but also impactful and responsible. As a project, 2Mynds started much earlier with the search for an optimal methodology for mental fitness.

The innovative concept at the heart of the company is that of mental fitness training based on training principles from exercise physiology. With an emphasis on prevention rather than therapy, 2Mynds is at the heart and start of a paradigm shift in mental health.

2Mynds is dedicated to helping society thrive at life by making mental fitness as ubiquitous as physical fitness. The technology to deliver on that promise is Flow 255®, 2Mynds' ecosystem for mental fitness, which can be accessed at www.2Mynds.com via monthly or yearly plans.

The 2Mynds brand was built on the idea that everything worthwhile requires effort and has humble beginnings. The logo is an abstract representation of a lotus - beautiful but growing from the mud. It has two outer boundaries, five petals on top, and five petals at the bottom, referring to the two states of mind, five mental skills, and five perspectives of Flow 255®.